MERRY CHRISTMAS

To DAD.

From PAUL, RACHEL &
ZACHARY.

A PICTORIAL
TREASURY OF
CLASSIC STEAM
TRAINS

A PICTORIAL TREASURY OF
CLASSIC STEAM
TRAINS

Nils Huxtable

BISON GROUP

First published in 1989 by
Bison Books Ltd
Kimbolton House
117 A Fulham Rd
London SW3 6RL

ISBN 0 86124 557 1
Printed and bound in Spain by Gráficas Estella, S.A. Navarra.
Printed in Spain

Page one: Leaving a billow of smoke behind it, Southern Pacific No 4449 charges out of Creswell, Oregon. *Page 2-3:* A Great Western 4-6-2 Pacific rounds a gentle curve near Stroud, England. *These pages:* A Union Pacific doubleheader with a 4-8-4 and a 4-6-6-4 providing the motive power.

All photos by Nils Huxtable

CONTENTS

INTRODUCTION 6

THE UNITED KINGDOM AND IRELAND 9

EUROPE AND THE SOVIET UNION 45

GREECE, TURKEY AND THE MIDDLE EAST 81

AFRICA 89

ASIA 109

AUSTRALIA 128

LATIN AMERICA 139

NORTH AMERICA 157

INDEX 192

INTRODUCTION

The steam locomotive is an important part of our industrial heritage. By the end of the nineteenth century, railroads were the principal means of communication and land transportation worldwide, and they became synonymous with progress and economic development. In the words of American poet Walt Whitman, the steam locomotive was the 'pulse of the continent.'

Nostalgically, the steam locomotive is often viewed as a marriage of art and technology, and surely no other machine has been the subject of, or featured in, so much literature or so many songs, paintings, films and photographs.

In many respects, modern steam technology never had a chance to prove itself against the diesel, which by 1960 had ousted steam traction from the main lines of the United States and Canada. The *Big Boy*, built in 1942, was hardly different—in principle—from Stephenson's *Rocket*, of 1825. But we tend to place greater value on things as they become scarce, and so it is with steam. Today, thousands line the tracks to see a locomotive like the *Daylight* 4-8-4 No 449, which three decades ago was but one of many.

Nowadays, of course, in order to find the steam locomotive in its 'natural' state, the photographer must travel beyond the limited—and artificial—realm of fan trips and into the wider world, where steam trains still perform the duties for which they were designed. In many developing nations, however, where the main priorities for most people are food and shelter, photography of steam engines must seem—even to the photographer himself at times—an irrelevant extravagance. Yet it is in such parts of the world that steam locomotives continue to operate in large numbers, so it is to Eastern Europe, South America, Africa and China that the cameraman must journey in order to record the passing of steam.

Unfortunately, the photographer in search of 'the real thing' may occasionally discover that his interest can be misinterpreted as something sinister. Pressing the shutter in front of a steam locomotive in a place like Yugoslavia, for example, where railroads are considered strategically important, is often followed by confiscation of film, arrest and interrogation. Such experiences serve to remind the cameraman that the steam locomotive has not only helped to build nations and empires, it has also been used to destroy them. Eastern Europe is a case in point.

To see the steam locomotive appreciated—even revered—as an *objet d'art*, one should come home again, or a little closer to home, for the appeal of steam is best understood in those parts of the industrialized world where it was first developed and where it has recently been retired from everyday employment. In Britain, North America, Western Europe, Australasia and Japan preservation has flourished. And the most realistic steam specimens are those that live.

The photographs in this album were taken over the last two decades of the steam locomotive, both in its 'special' role as a working museum exhibit and as a workhorse in regular service. Some chapters are devoted to preserved steam locomotives exclusively; others show them in their final—and not necessarily finest—hours: neglected and run-down. In this way, perhaps, steam's decline and revival can be seen as simultaneous trends, and since the selection of illustrations is contemporary, they may seem more meaningful.

This, then, is the world of the steam as seen through the eyes of someone who finds a 4-6-2 Pacific in China and a 4-6-6-4 Challenger in Wyoming equally fascinating.

Reminders of a bygone era—*Below:* **SL 620 roars out of Changchun and UP 3985 crosses the vast plains of the United States** *at right*.

THE UNITED KINGDOM AND IRELAND

I t seems only fitting that a pictorial survey of world steam should begin in Britain, where the steam locomotive was invented and where the first seeds of preservation have grown into an impressive forest of schemes stretching across the country.

In 1960 there were still 10,000 steam engines in operation on the railways of the United Kingdom and Ireland. However, the pell-mell dieselization of British Railways—particularly the scrapping of steam power and the radical pruning of the system—combined to bring about the abrupt end of an era in just eight short years. The response to this wasteful destruction was the preservation movement, which sought to save not only locomotives and rolling stock but the railways themselves and an entire way of life. Though many interesting examples have been lost forever, enough remains today of these 'emblems of motion and power' to remind us of the not-so-distant past, and the great age of trains.

The 0-6-0 tender engine was one of the most popular types in the British Isles. The standard freight locomotive for the Lancashire & Yorkshire Railway, the Barton Wright 0-6-0, was introduced in 1876; however, most of the 280 built were converted into saddle tanks. Of the remaining 50, No 52044, which lasted as a works shunter at Crewe until the 1960s, is the only survivor. It is shown (*opposite*) wearing its L&Y number, at Steamtown Carnforth.

The Midland Railway also built 0-6-0s in considerable numbers between 1876 and 1922, and the London Midland & Scottish Railway, of which both the L&Y and the MR became a part, continued construction until 1942. Although used principally for freight work, these engines could show a good turn of speed on local passenger services and excursions.

In Ireland, too, the 0-6-0 found favor, being employed until the end of regular steam operation. Still at work on excursions during the 1980s is former Great Southern & Western No 186 (*below*) built in 1879.

Built to replace the old Dean Goods 0-6-0s, 120 of these taper boiler variants were constructed by the Great Western Railway beginning in 1930. The last survivor of the 2251 Class is No 3205, shown here in a bucolic setting near Eardington, on the Severn Valley Railway.

Most useful and ubiquitous of all shunting engines was the 0-6-0 tank. On the Midland Railway, locomotives of this type began to appear in 1874. The same design, virtually unchanged apart from a Belpaire Boiler and an enclosed cab, was perpetuated by the LMS. In all, more than 400 were constructed between 1924 and 1931. These engines, nicknamed 'Jinties,' endured until the last year of steam on British Railways. At Haworth, on the Keighley & Worth Valley Railway (*opposite*), No 47279 (*on the right*) keeps company with a GI 2-8-0 that was purchased in Sweden.

The Great Western also built hundreds of tank engines with the 0-6-0 wheel arrangement, preferring rounded saddle or pannier tanks to carry water. Use of these locomotives began as early as 1860, and some had outside frames. A standard design of 0-6-0 was adopted in 1929, and by the time construction ceased in 1956, more than 1000 0-6-0s of all classes were in service, being used for shunting, banking, hauling loose-coupled coal and freight trains, and working cross-country and branch line locals. No 3738 (*opposite, below*) belongs to the Great Western Society at Didcot.

One of the smallest groups of 0-6-0s was the South Eastern & Chatham Railway's P Class, of which only eight were built in 1909 and 1910. They were intended for branch line push-pull service, and four have been saved for posterity. One of them, shown in its British Railways guise as No 31556 (*this page*), operates on the Kent & East Sussex Railway.

By the late nineteenth century, the 4-4-0 had gained universal acceptance in both Britain and Ireland as the principal main line passenger engine. Despite heavier train weights and the introduction of more powerful locomotives, 4-4-0s continued to find work on less exacting duties, usually on secondary and cross-country routes. Two examples of turn-of-the-century 4-4-0s are the London & South Western Railway T9 of 1899 and the Great Western Railway City Class of 1903. The T9s totaled 66 engines. Nicknamed 'greyhounds,' they were favorites on expresses between Salisbury and Exeter. In their latter days they could be seen on short distance stopping trains in the Southwest. Wearing the handsome British Railways lined black, mixed traffic livery, the last survivor, No 30120 (*opposite*) nears Ropley on the Mid-Hants Railway.

No 3440 *City of Truro* of 1903 (*below*) represents the transition period in Great Western locomotive development, since outside frames and a taper boiler were used in its construction. In 1903 it became the first steam locomotive to reach 100 miles per hour. Withdrawn from service in 1931, it has been restored to service twice—in 1957 and again in 1985—the latter occasion for the 150th anniversary of the Great Western Railway.

To the Southern Railway must go the credit for the world's most advanced 4-4-0. Built as a lightweight, abbreviated Lord Nelson (*see page 25*) for express work on restricted routes, the 40 Schools Class locomotives appeared between 1930 and 1935. Almost as powerful as the King Arthur 4-6-0s (*see pages 25-27*), they could handle heavy expresses with ease. One of the class, No 926 *Repton*, became part of the Steamtown collection in Vermont. On the *right* is the Bluebell Railway's No 928 *Stowe*.

The 2-6-0, or Mogul type, gained acceptance as a lightweight general purpose engine on all of Britain's 'Big Four' railways. One of the most modern Moguls, introduced just after nationalization, was the London & North Eastern Railway's K-1, designed by AH Peppercorn as a two-cylinder version of Sir Nigel Gresley's K-4. No 62005 (*above*), wearing the LNER apple green livery it never wore in regular service, is shown at work on the North Yorkshire Moors Railway.

Following World War II, the LMS introduced a lightweight 2-6-0 for work on cross-country routes and branches. Construction continued after nationalization and British Railways adopted both the LMS 4MT 2-6-0 (exemplified by No 43106 *below*) and the 2-6-2T version as standard designs, with minor modifications. One of the British Railway Standard Moguls, No 76017, is shown *opposite*. Parts were interchangeable with other Standard classes.

Designer BG Ivatt's smaller Mogul design of 1946 was also adopted by British Railways as a standard class. No 46443 is seen on the Severn Valley Railway, on the kind of branch line passenger train for which it was so admirably suited.

Surely no other railway in Britain depended on the 4-6-0 as much as the Great Western Railway. The first 4-6-0, intended solely for express passenger work, appeared in 1902. The two-cylinder version, known as the Saint Class, was the forerunner of the prolific Halls and Modified Halls, which became general purpose engines, as did the Granges and Manors—4-6-0 versions of a highly successful class of 2-6-0s. One of the early Halls, No 4930 *Hagley* is seen passing Standish Junction (*left*) with a Great Western 150 excursion. The aforementioned classes were all named for stately residences in parts of the country served by the Great Western Railway.

No 7819 *Hinton Manor* (*below*) was photographed one winter evening at Bewdley, on the Severn Valley Railway.

The more powerful four-cylinder Star Class 4-6-0, introduced for express work by designer GJ Chruchward in 1906, was further developed by his successor, Charles Collett, resulting in the famous Castles and Kings. During the 1950s, some of the Castles, such as No 7029 *Clun Castle* (*opposite*), and all the Kings were fitted with double blast pipes and four-row superheaters. Despite the improved performance of the modified engines, all were withdrawn by the mid-1960s, when diesels replaced them.

First of the Kings, No 6000 *King George V*, gained fame early in its career when it toured the United States. The engine, normally based at Bulmer's of Hereford, who sponsored its return to service, was also the first steam locomotive to operate on British Railway tracks in 1971 after the notorious ban on main line steam operation was lifted.

On other railways besides the Great Western, the 4-6-0 was the mainstay of main line and secondary services, hauling everything from crack expresses to local freights. The Southern Railway's first modern express 4-6-0 was the King Arthur Class, named for the Knights of the Round Table and other characters associated with the mythical kingdom of Camelot. So successful were the first 20 designed by Urie for the London & South Western Railway in 1918, additional orders for 54 more slightly improved engines followed, of which No 777 *Sir Lamiel* (*opposite*) was one.

An express freight variant, with smaller diameter wheels, appeared in 1920. One of these, No 506, is shown on *this page* climbing Medstead Bank with a Mid-Hants Railway Santa Special.

Largest of the Southern Railway 4-6-0s was the Lord Nelson Class, introduced in 1926 for working the heavy Continental boat trains, duties for which they were still occasionally employed in 1962, their final year of British Railway services. Class leader No 850 (*opposite, below*) was being cleaned at Carnforth in August 1985.

Sir Lamiel in full cry near Seer Green. The last surviving King Arthur and now part of the National Railway Museum collection housed at York, No 777 was one of the engines rostered for Marylebone-High Wycome Santa Specials during the winter of 1986-87.

One of Sir William Stanier's most highly acclaimed designs for the LMS, the Black Five 4-6-0 was introduced in 1934 as a general purpose engine. Considered one of the most reliable and efficient classes ever to run on Britain's railways, there were 842 in service by 1950, and were equally at home on heavy expresses or pick-up freights. No 5305 (*below*) has found a new career as an excursion engine. The magnificent York station, with is ornate overall roof, is the setting for this picture, showing No 5305 on a *Scarborough Spa Express*.

Stanier's express passenger 4-6-0 of the Jubilee Class had three cylinders and larger driving wheels than their mixed traffic cousins. Painted maroon in pre-war LMS days, many were given names associated with the British Empire. No 5690 *Leander* (*opposite*) was photographed at Steamtown Carnforth.

LMS locomotive design had a direct influence on the British Railway Standard locomotive classes introduced after nationalization. With smaller wheels and boilers than both the LMS and BR Class 5 4-6-0s, the 75000 series 4-6-0 of 1951 was given a 4MT power rating. Shown *at right* is No 75078, the penultimate member of the Class, photographed at Haworth, on the Keighley & Worth Valley Railway.

The first 2-8-0, or Consolidation, in Britain was built by Great Western Railway in 1903. Used on heavy coal and freight trains, a few survived until 1965. No 2857, shown at Newport in 1985 (*opposite*), was rescued from a Barry scrap yard.

Although the Midland Railway constructed no freight engines larger than an 0-6-0 for its own purposes, it did produce a very handsome 2-8-0 design for the Somerset and Dorset Joint Railway. The 11 engines of the class, including No 13809 (*below*), now preserved at the Midland Railway Centre, were responsible for hauling freight trains over the steep grades between Bournemouth and Bath, until they were withdrawn from service in the early 1960s.

So successful were Sir William Stanier's 8F 2-8-0s of 1935 that they were adopted by the War Department as a standard freight engine for use in Britain and abroad. In this latter capacity they served in Iran, Egypt and Turkey. Built in large numbers at the principal workshops of all four pre-nationalization railways, they lasted until the end of stream operation on British Railway in 1968. In Turkey, a handful have survived into the 1980s. No 8233 (*left*) saw service in Iran, returned to Britain in 1952 and, after a few years on the Longmoor Military Railway, became British Railway's No 48773 in 1957.

Although already a proven performer in the United States and elsewhere, the 4-6-2, or Pacific, did not gain prominence as a powerful express passenger locomotive in Britain until 1922. As early as 1908, the Great Western Railway had introduced its Great Bear Pacific, but weight restrictions precluded its use on any route except the London-Bristol main line, and the engine was rebuilt as a Castle 4-6-0 (*see page 21*). LNER Chief Mechanical Engineer Sir Nigel Gresley designed the three-cylinder A3 (originally A1) 4-6-2, including the world famous *Flying Scotsman* (*opposite*). The engines of this class worked principally on the East Coast

main line until dieselization began to thin their ranks in 1960-61.

An improved, streamlined version of the A3 appeared in 1935 to haul the new, high speed *Silver Jubilee* and *Coronation* expresses. In 1938 No 4468 *Mallard* (*below*) reached 126 mph, the highest speed ever recorded for a steam locomotive.

No 4498 (*above*) was named for its designer. *Mallard* was withdrawn from service in 1962, and was exhibited at Clapham until the National Railway Museum was established at York. *Sir Nigel Gresley* spent the last years of its British Railway career in Scotland and was not taken out of service until 1966.

Between its transoceanic trips to the United States in 1969 and to Australia in 1988, *Flying Scotsman* is a long-standing favorite for excursions on British Railway tracks. As seen here, No 4472 was galloping past the golf course at Seer Green, on the former Great Western Paddington-Birmingham main line in December 1986.

The Princess Royal Class Pacific was Sir William Stanier's first design as newly appointed Chief Mechanical Engineer of the LMS. Built to haul expresses over the West Coast main line, which features some steep grades north of Crewe, the 4-6-2s had Swindon-type taper boilers, and one of the class, No 6202, was constructed as a turbine-driven locomotive. Virtually destroyed in the Harrow accident of 1952, it was the first Princess Royal to be scrapped. The remaining 12 lasted until dieselization 10 years later, and two have been preserved. No 6201 *Princess Elizabeth* (*this page and opposite*) is based at Bulmer's Cider Factory in Hereford.

An improved Stanier Pacific, the Coronation Class, entered service in 1937. The first 10 constructed were fully streamlined, but the casing was later removed for ease of maintenance. Class leader No 6220 achieved a maximum speed of 114 mph on test, and No 46229 *Duchess of Hamilton* (*opposite, below*) toured the United States in 1939, disguised as No 6220. All 38 engines were eventually fitted with smoke deflectors and double blast pipes, and three have been preserved.

Compared to the climb to Shap on the West Coast Main Line, the slight gradient east of Leeds is easy sailing for a powerful locomotive like *Duchess of Hamilton*. Wearing smart British Railway maroon livery and latter day British Railway No 46229, the Pacific makes light work of the *Scarborough Spa Express* near Cross Gates.

Pacifics on the Southern Railway, meanwhile, did not appear until the World War II. Designed by OV Bulleid, these new three-cylinder 4-6-2s, both heavy and lightweight versions, featured thermic syphons, chain-drive valve gear and air-smooth casings. Beginning in 1956, the heavier Merchant Navy Class, including the No 35028 *Clan Line* engine (*opposite, below*), were rebuilt with Walschaerts valve gear, and the streamlining was removed. About half of the Battle of Britain and West Country Pacifics were similarly dealt with from 1957 on, with the rest retaining their shrouding. No 34092 *City of Wells* (*below*) is an unmodified engine; No 34016 *Bodmin* (*opposite*) is a rebuilt, although the former was recently fitted with a Giesl ejector to improve performance.

Unlike the railroads of North America and elsewhere, the nationalized railways of Britain did not begin to dieselize until well into the 1950s. Instead, a plan for 12 standard designs was adopted in 1950, with a view to replacing life-expired steam power systemwide. By the time 9F Class 2-10-0 No 92220 *Evening Star* rolled out of Swindon locomotive factory 10 years later, only 999 standard engines were in service, hardly enough to make a difference in the overall efficiency of the steam fleet.

Withdrawn after a working life of only five years, *Evening Star*, the last steam locomotive built for British Railways, represents the best of the Standard designs. Generally used on coal, ore and fitted freight trains, the 9Fs were occasionally called upon to power express passenger trains, and speeds of 90 mph have been recorded.

The smaller of two intermediate mixed traffic, or general service, Standard 4-6-0 Classes was the 75000 series, which appeared three years before the 9F of 1954. No 75027 (*left*), which saw service on the former Cambrian lines of the old Great Western, has been painted Swindon green. No 75078 (*featured on page 29*) wears British Railway lined black and is fitted with a double chimney.

The passenger tank version of the Standard 4-6-0 was the 80000 series 2-6-4T, based on a large group of 545 similar engines built by the LMS (and later British Railways) with few modifications. Like their predecessors, the 155 standard tank engines were intended for suburban, express and branch passenger trains. The last to be constructed appeared in 1957. No 80079 (*opposite*) awaits departure from Bridnorth, on the Severn Valley Railway.

EUROPE AND THE SOVIET UNION

As in Britain and the United States, the streamlining trend of the 1930s also influenced Belgian locomotive design. Six 12 Class 4-4-2 Atlantics entered service in 1938 on fast trains between Brussels and Ostend. These exotic engines had bar frames and inside cylinders, and were the last express locomotives built for the Belgian State Railways (SNCB). No 12.004 (*opposite*) was returned to active duty in 1985 in time to celebrate 150 years of railways in Belgium.

Compounding was undoubtedly the greatest influence of steam locomotive development in France. André Chapelon, one of the world's finest locomotive engineers, increased the power output of many older 4-6-2s and then employed similar principles of using the same steam twice in the construction of new 2-8-2s, 4-8-2s and 2-10-0s. The first 4-8-2 was built in France; so was the last: the graceful four-cylinder compound 241P (*below*). Intended for main line express work, the 35 engines of this class were soon displaced by electrification and dieselization.

However, it was the simpler, more rugged 2-8-2s of American and Canadian manufacture that sang the swan song of steam in France. More than 1300 Mikados arrived after World War II o aid in the recovery of the war-ravaged French National Railroads (SNCF). Here, five oil-burners are lined up outside the Cerbère roundhouse (*right*), while a diesel lurks in the background.

If compounding was the answer to improved locomotive performance in France, the Franco-Crosti boiler, as fitted to a 2-8-0 (*opposite*) was the innovation applied to lower the fuel consumption of many engines belonging to the Italian State Railways (FS). Although steam development in Italy ceased as early as 1930, a handful of steam locomotives survived into the 1980s. One of them was this 0-6-0 rack tank engine, No 981.003 (*above*), which operated on the branch line between Paola and Cosenza until recently.

The 940 Class 2-8-2T appeared in 1921. Basically a tank engine version of the ubiquitous standard 740 Class 2-8-0 freight locomotive, the 940 was used for branch line goods and passenger work. No 940.038 (*below*) was at Villazano, in Northern Italy, with a ballast train in 1974.

For years the 5-foot, 6-inch gauge Spanish State Railway (RENFE) was the 'sick man of Europe,' with an inefficient, but incredibly diverse, collection of locomotives and add-on components. Garratts, Mallets and shuffling centenarians made Spain a paradise for the steam fan. The situation changed very rapidly, however, and by 1975 the RENFE had achieved complete dieselization, with electrification proceeding apace.

Memories of steam's latter days in Spain are shown here. The 4-8-0 was a favored wheel arrangement on Spanish railways, and the design illustrated was ordered by three pre-nationalization companies, and later by the RENFE itself. This 240F 2475 (*below*) was at Salamanca in January 1971.

Only 10 of the big 242F Class 4-8-4s were built in 1956 for express work on the non-electrified sections of the Irun-Madrid main line. Though few in number, the class survived until the end of steam traction in Spain, but by 1974 No 2008 (*above*) had been reduced to freight chores between Miranda and Zaragoza.

The 2-8-2 type was popular with the RENFE, and nearly 300 Mikados were built in Britain and Spain between 1953 and 1960. Excellent general purpose engines, they were used on heavy freight and express trains all over the system. Locomotive No 141F 2111 (*opposite*) has been retained in working order for special trains, and in this capacity it is shown erupting oil smoke at Coscurita, enroute from Soria to Madrid.

No 2111 again, this time doubleheading with a German-built 4-8-4T named *Escatron*, blackens the blue skies over Gomara Almenar, between Soria and Calatayud. The occasion is a fan trip organized by the Locomotive Club of Great Britain.

Like Spain, Portugal was a veritable museum for steam power. By the 1970s, both meter and broad gauge steam locomotives were concentrated in the north of the country, and it was here that they lived out their final years, appreciated more by British steam fans starved for 'the real thing' than by the Portuguese themselves. Imagine riding a meter gauge suburban (serving the city of Oporto) pulled by a four-cylinder compound 0-4-4-0T Mallets (*below*), built by Henschel in 1908! Or the venerable

inside-cylinder broad gauge 4-6-0s like the one *above* at Tua in the Douro Valley. British enthusiasts nicknamed these engines 'B-12s' for the Great Eastern Railway 4-6-0s they resembled.

Then there are the equally handsome 2-6-4s of Swiss design (*opposite*), intended for suburban and semi-fast services. Though nearing the end of their working lives, the steam locomotives of the Portuguese Railway Company (CP) were beautifully maintained, often with polished brass and copper trim.

On a winter morning, fog lifts from the Douro Valley in Portu- as a meter gauge train, pulled by a Henschel 2-4-6-0T Mallet, sses the dual gauge bridge over the Corgo River.

Despite the country's mountainous terrain, Swiss Federal Railways (SBB) never owned anything larger than a 2-10-0. More typical of Swiss steam is this handsome Eb3/5 series 2-6-2T (*opposite*) kept by the SBB for excursions. With most railways electrified by 1930, steam's role in Switzerland was limited. Thus, SBB steam locomotives had to be both uncomplicated and reliable.

Austrian steam certainly was not handsome, but its development, beginning with compounding and other innovations introduced by State Railways (OBB) Chief Mechanical Engineer Karl Golsdorf in 1893, continued for six decades, culminating in 1951 with the fuel-efficient Giesl ejector, which has been fitted to locomotives all over the world. Two major wars resulted in the dispersal of many Austrian engines to other countries and the need to import locomotives of foreign manufacture. Among the last steam engines to operate on the OBB were German Kriegslok 2-10-0s, many of which were Austrian-built. Representative of lightweight branch line power is turn-of-the-century two-cylinder compound 2-6-0T No 91.107 (*opposite, below*) shown doubleheading with a 92 Class 0-8-0T. Austria's narrow gauge lines gave it the distinction of being one of the last Western European countries to feature regular steam operation. Now a tourist railway, the 760 mm gauge line from Garsten to Grunberg is operated by delightful 0-6-2Ts like No 298.25 (*this page*).

Until 1972, when steam power was officially withdrawn from active duty, the Swedish State Railways (SJ) kept a number of locomotives in reserve against a shortage of diesels or electrics, which were vulnerable to severe winter conditions. In this stand-by role, steam could be found shunting at major depots or hauling an extra freight. Nowadays, a strong preservation movement in Sweden ensures the occasional steam trip, even on electrified lines. On such an assignment was this Halsingbörg-Hasselehölm Railway inside-cylinder 4-6-0 (*this page*) at Klippan. With few exceptions, most Swedish engines were home-built.

Because of its relatively flat topography, Denmark never had any need for superpower steam locomotives. In fact, the State Railways' (DSB) largest passenger locomotives were compound Pacifics purchased secondhand from Sweden. A lack of coal,

together with hard water, put steam at a disadvantage in Denmark, and regular operation had ceased by 1970. Typical of branch line steam power in Denmark is D2 Class 2-6-0 No 826 (*opposite*). The metal band around the chimney bears the national colors of red and white.

Since Norway, like Denmark, was dependent on imported coal, the fuel efficiency of steam locomotives was of prime importance. Thus, compounding was employed extensively in engines used by the Norwegian State Railways (NSB). Other limitations were placed on locomotives because of Norway's mountainous terrain, and the system was an early candidate for full dieselization and electrification. For main line work, eight driving wheels were the rule. One of Norway's preserved engines, two-cylinder 2-8-0 No 236 (*opposite, below*) heads a special train at Krøderen in 1980.

Coal was also scarce in Finland where oil, wood or even peat was used as fuel for the steam locomotives of the Finnish State Railways (VR). Simple but robust, a pleasing blend of German and North American practice, VR steam survived into the 1970s, becoming particularly active during the winter months, when the country's northern ports were frozen. The largest group of locomotives on the roster was the Tk3 2-8-0, (*above*) which could traverse the most lightly laid of branch lines. This VR3 Class heavy 0-10-0T No 754 (*below*) was one of five built in 1924 and 1926 for yard shunting.

A bird's eye view of Kouvola roundhouse (*right*) shows Tr-1 2-8-2 No 1094 and other members of a class completed as recently as 1957. Mixed traffic engines, the 67 Tr-1s had boilers interchangeable with those of a similar-looking group of Pacifics. As in Sweden, a few hundred Finnish steam locomotives were mothballed as part of a strategic reserve.

Given the political division of the country, it would seem logical to divide the locomotive fleets of the German Federal Railways (DB) and its Eastern counterpart (DR). Very little new steam locomotive construction for either system occurred after World War II; instead, rebuilding was the rule. Many classes were common to both Germanys, while a few engine groups became unique to one side or the other because of scrapping and reassignment of locomotives.

Found only on the DB were the fabulous 01.10 series three-cylinder Pacifics (*opposite*). Introduced as a standard DR design in 1939 (Germany's standardization program had begun 15 years before), these 4-6-2s were the most powerful DB express passenger engines, with the exception of the two short-lived 10 Class Pacifics built in 1956. All the 01.10s were rebuilt from 1951 on, with larger, welded boilers. Most were oil-fired, and they were capable of spectacular performances, particularly on the main lines radiating from Hamburg.

The last steam locomotive built for the DB in 1959 was 23 Class 2-6-2 No 23.105 (*left*), one of 105 intended as replacements for the delightful ex-Prussian Railways (KPEV) P8 4-6-0 (*below*). Between 1906 and 1924 around 3850 of these 'maids-of-all-work' were constructed for use at home and in countries such as Poland and Romania (*see pages 69 and 73*). Others were transferred as war reparations to Germany's neighbors. East Germany's P8s (Class 38.10) lasted until 1972; West Germany's until 1975.

Two former Prussian Railways designs found only on the DR during the 1970s, by which time they had been retired on the DB, were the 95 Class 2-10-2T (*opposite*) and the three-cylinder 58.10 Class 2-10-0 (*below*). The latter, known as the G12, was the first German standard type, and the DR rebuilt 56 with welded boilers, new cylinders, valve gears, cabs and tenders.

Another of the DR's more interesting features was a dwindling network of steam-worked narrow gauge lines, some operated by such charming favorites as the Saxon-Meyer 0-4-4-0T Mallets. Seen here, No 99.1585 (*above*) was shunting at Steinbach in 1982. The first of these 96 engines was built by Hartmann of Chemnitz (now Karl Marx-Stadt) for the Saxon State Railways in 1882.

Between 1926 and 1937 the DR built 241 heavy Pacifics for express work. The postwar survivors were allocated to depots on each side of the east-west border, and both the DB and the DR, each in its own way, extensively rebuilt a considerable number before dieselization halted the program. This meant that three distinctly different versions of the 01 resulted: original, DB rebuilt and DR rebuilt.

One of the originals, with small Witte-type smoke deflectors, leaves the Bavarian town of Neuenmarkt-Wirsberg on a stopping train for Hof, near the border with East Germany and Czechoslovakia. In regular service, the DR 01s outlasted by eight years those on the DB, which were retired in 1973.

Of all the Eastern bloc countries, only Poland continued using steam in quantity through the 1980s. Attempts by the Polish State Railways (PKP) to effect reconstruction and organization of an assortment of different gauges and locomotive types inherited from Prussia, Austria and Russia was disrupted by World War II, which left the PKP in shambles. Postwar assistance by the United States included 100 heavy freight 2-10-0s built by Alco, Baldwin and Lima (*this page*). Beginning in 1948 Polish locomotive factories supplied 180 Pt 47 Class 2-8-2s (*opposite*) for express duties on non-electrified main lines. Among the Polish designs, the Pt 47s endured until the late 1980s. A number of veteran Prussian P8 4-6-0s, classed Ok 1 by the PKP, outlived their brethren in East and West Germany by five years. Two of them (*opposite, below*) are shown at the Miedzyrzecz roundhouse in the summer of 1979.

The influence of French locomotive development under André Chapelon was put into practice on the postwar State Railways of Czechoslovakia (CSD) which, like the Polish Railways, had made an attempt at organizing and modernizing its varied fleet, only to have its efforts thwarted by the ravages of war. Older CSD freight power is represented by 2-8-0 No 434.2218 (*opposite*). The design originated in Austria and was developed by the Czechs. The dry-steam pipe connecting the two domes does not enhance the appearance of this homely-looking specimen, however.

Postwar steam development in Czechoslovakia reached its zenith with the introduction of the 498.1 series three-cylinder 4-8-2 express locomotive of 1954-55 (*opposite, below*) and the 556.0 Class 2-10-0 freight engine of 1952-57 (*this page*). The best of German and French locomotive engineering was incorporated into these two designs, the last to be produced for the CSD by the famous Skoda factory. The red star fitted to the smokebox of each locomotive illustrated was a characteristic of Czechoslovakian steampower.

Most of the steam locomotives of the Bulgarian State Railways (BDZ) were of German design. Modern types included three-cylinder 2-8-4Ts, 2-12-4Ts, 2-8-2s and 4-8-2s, but it was the ex-Reichsbahn 2-10-0 (*left*) that closed the chapter on steam in Bulgaria.

Romania was another Eastern Bloc country whose railway system was affected by war and the consequent acquisition and loss of territory. Fifty-two classes came from Hungary alone, but those adopted by the State Railways (CFR) as standard were of Austrian and German design. These included the magnificent 142 Class 2-8-4 (*below*), built in Romania between 1937 and 1940 as copies of the Austrian 214 Class.

The well-loved P8 (*opposite*) was purchased, both from the Prussian State Railways (KPEV) and the German State Railways, and then duplicated in Romania itself, for a total of 376 engines. An interesting feature of many Romanian and Bulgarian steam locomotives was the Romanian innovation of dual firing. The tender carried both a coal bunker and an oil tank. Coal was used when the engine was not working hard, oil when conditions were more difficult.

As part of the Austro-Hungarian Empire, Hungary quite naturally employed the ideas of Austrian designers at first. However, war changed not only the map of Hungary but also the motive and power requirements of the State Railways (MAV). Mountainous territory was lost to Romania and Yugoslavia, and along with it, entire classes of powerful Mallets. Many of the more unusual types built in Hungary between the wars, including four streamlined 4-4-4Ts, had been retired well before the last decade of regular steam operation, but there was considerable variety to be found, both on the MAV and on industrial railways, with engines ranging from the sublime to the impudent. The 424 Class 4-8-0 (*right*) is considered one of the most successful designs ever built, and many were exported to Yugoslavia, the Soviet Union and other countries. The outside-frame 0-6-0T of classical antiquity (*opposite*) was still working at a sugar factory near Budapest in 1979. No fewer than 488 of these diminutive shunters were built between 1885 and 1909.

In 1918 the newly constituted railways of Yugoslavia (SHS, later JĎZ) were burdened with a motley assortment of locomotives, inherited mainly from Serbia, Austria and Hungary. Only three types—4-6-2, 2-8-2 and 2-10-2—were designed specifically for Yugoslavia, and these arrived from Germany between the wars. After World War II the situation was even more confused, with locomotives from six more countries added to the JĎZ roster. The variety of standard and narrow gauge engines in Yugoslavia was exciting, and so was photographing them, since anyone found putting a beauty like the ex-Serbian Railways' 2-6-2 (*below*) on film was subject to arrest.

Another country where railways were militarily important—and where photographing steam locomotives was automatically suspect—was the Soviet Union. By 1970 steam's share of the tonnage there was less than 10 percent and many of the Soviet Railways' large (SZD) steam locomotives—2-10-2s and 2-8-4s—had already been sold to China or retired. However, large, strategic reserves of steam power existed all over the country, and in an emergency, hundreds of 2-10-0s or 0-10s-0s could be made ready for service in 24 hours.

But what of regularly active steam? Relatively scarce, difficult to find and risky to photograph. Postwar acquisitions of locomotives from neighboring countries were scrapped relatively early in favor of standard designs like the E Class 0-10-0, of which no fewer than 10,000 were constructed. Even the dinky P9 0-6-0T (*above*) was produced in large numbers—an estimated 2000 between 1936 and 1957.

The total for the L Class lightweight 2-10-0 (*below*) was more than 5000, and the number of S and Su 2-6-2 passenger locomotives (*right*), built over a 40 year period beginning in 1910 exceeded 3700–almost the same production figure as that for the Prussian P8. The Su Prairies handled most passenger trains—from main line to branch line—prior to electrification and dieselization.

The star of Soviet steam—the hauntingly beautiful P36 4-8-4—was duplicated only 250 times, and the photographer who set out to track them down in their waning years had to travel to the Soviet Far East, beyond Lake Baikal, where they had been drafted following electrification of the main lines radiating from Moscow. The passenger on the Moscow-Vladivostok *Rossiya* express would be rewarded, beginning on the fifth day of travel, with relays of these fabulous 4-8-4s, the last new steam locomotives built for main service in the Soviet Union. No 0189, its drivers encrusted with ice, waits to depart Skovorodino with the westbound *Rossiya* in December 1972.

GREECE, TURKEY AND THE MIDDLE EAST

The last years of steam in Greece were like the death of the protagonist in a Greek tragedy—painful and protracted. Even before World War II, the Hellenic State Railways had acquired a muddled collection of locomotives from a variety of builders. Postwar requirements were satisfied by the delivery of US Army 0-6-0Ts (*opposite*) and 2-8-0s, together with 2-10-0s from Baldwin and the British War Department. But the most unusual engines of all were ordered new from Italy, which had no experience in building modern steam. The result was the massive Ma 2-10-2 (*opposite, below*), a monster which never performed satisfactorily. Motive power shortages were temporarily relieved

by borrowing engines from Austria and even France. In Greece, it was inevitable that the *deus ex machina* be a diesel.

Turkey, by contrast, kept its steam fleet going into the 1980s. The private companies that by 1936 had become the Turkish State Railways (TCUD) contributed an array of British-, French- and German-built engines, but it was mainly to Germany that the TCUD turned for subsequent power and the ubiquitous 2-10-0 in particular. German-designed but Czech-built was Decapod No 56160 (*this page*), seen climbing to Soğanli with a freight in October 1982. The last two locomotives in this class were built in the TCUD Sivas and Eskisehir workshops.

Among the American contributions to the TCUD roster were some standard US Army 2-8-0s of 1943, Middle East 2-8-2s of 1942 (*above*) and 88 heavy, 2-10-0s, which came from Vulcan Iron Works in 1947 and 1948 (*below*). The Mikados were used as motive power for freight, long-distance passenger and even suburban trains, whereas the 2-10-0s were employed almost exclusively on freight.

The only express passenger engines built for the TCUD were a small group of 11 2-8-2s, supplied by Henschel in 1937. At Konya, where the graceful Mikados ran out their final miles, No 46057 (*opposite*) is having its firebox cleaned.

A favorite location for photographers in Turkey was the great curving viaduct at Eğridir. Here, the blue waters of Lake Eğridir serve as a canvas on which a Prussian G8 type 0-8-0 is seen painting with smoky gray brush strokes.

By the mid-1970s, steam operations had come to an end on the standard gauge railways of Syria, although new standard gauge lines were still under construction. For steam the photographer had to look to the capital, Damascus, terminus of the fabled narrow gauge Hedjaz Railway. The through train to Amman was hauled by a Hartmann 2-8-2 *(opposite, below)* as far as the Jordanian border, where a Japanese-built Pacific of the Royal Jordanian Railways *(opposite)* took over. When the Jordanians had asked the United States for new motive power in the 1950s, they specified *steam,* and only Japan could fill the order.

With the Lebanese border effectively closed because of guerilla activity and the Damascus-Beirut line severed in places, service had beeen cut back to Sergayah, inside Syria. Shown *below,* 0-4-4-2T No 962 heads the daily train along what has become little more than a branch.

AFRICA

To the steam photographer, Africa means Garratts, those extraordinary double locomotives with a water tender in front, coal (or oil) supplies at the rear and the boiler in between. For the 3-foot, 6-inch gauge (or in the case of East Africa, meter gauge) railways of the continent, the Garratt, more efficient than, but just as powerful as, other articulateds of comparable size, was the answer to steep grades, sharp curves, and in many cases, lightly-laid track.

On the main line between the great port city of Mambassa and the capital city of Nairobi, 59 Class 4-8-2 + 2-8-4 No 5926 *Mount Kimhanda* (*opposite*), supplied by master Garratt builder Beyer Peacock in 1955, slams away from Voi under a cloud of oil smoke with freight for Nairobi.

Garratts did not fare well in all the African countries that owned them, however. Sudan, for example, sold its 4-6-4 + 4-6-4s to Rhodesia in 1949, opting instead for prewar designs like the 220 Class Pacific (*below*) shown in very run-down condition near Sennar Junction.

In Ghana, meanwhile, Garratts were retired by diesels, which by the mid-1970s were themselves being set aside because of a shortage of spares. This 0-8-0T shunter No 23 (*right*), built in the 1930s, was one of the few steam locomotives still capable of turning a wheel in 1976.

Zimbabwe is one of the few countries in Africa where steam has a bright future, and the National Railway of Zimbabwe (NRZ) steam fleet consists almost entirely of Garratts. Indeed, Zimbabwe is remarkable in that steam locomotives are replacing diesels on some lines. Instead of sinking further into debt by dieselizing completely as many other African countries have done, Zimbabwe has embarked on a program of limited electrification, while refurbishing most of its steam engines and even buying others secondhand.

In 1976 Bulawayo shed was host to Garratts of four different classes. In the scene *opposite*, 14th Class Hudson Garratt No 419

from Beyer Peacock, developed in 1940, was being serviced alongside a 1930 15th Class Prairie Garratt No 518, also by Beyer Peacock. On the West Nicholson branch, 16th Class Mikado Garratt No 612 (*opposite, below*) while its crew is being protected by the military against possible terrorist attack.

Most impressive of all NRZ Garratts is the 20/20A Class Mountain Garratt supplied by Beyer Peacock in 1954. Stating the case for locomotives that burn what they haul, 20A 4-8-2 + 2-8-4 No 749 storms around a curve on the Victoria Falls line with a load of Hwange coal (*below*).

With plentiful coal resources and the industrial capacity for manufacturing its own locomotives, South Africa would seem like a perfect setting for modern steam power, whether Garratts or more conventional types. Unfortunately, politics and not economics have dominated the policies of South African Railways (SAR), and steam is being retired at a rapid rate.

The British school of locomotive development in South Africa is represented by the locomotives on these two pages. The 10CR Class Pacific, built by North British in 1910 (*opposite*), was intended for passenger service, but spent the remaining years of its SAR career as a Cape Town shunter. Sold to a gold mining concern, it still had a few miles left on it when photographed in 1983.

One of Chief Mechanical Engineer DA Hendrie's first designs was his 15/15A 4-8-2, which first appeared in 1914. The majority of these engines were rebuilt with larger boilers during the Depression, and No 2092 (*this page*), shown leaving Queenstown with an excursion, is one of the 4-8-2s so modified. Dating from the same period and also rebuilt in 12AR Class is 4-8-2 No 1535 (*opposite, below*), here being prepared for a rail tour at Germiston, near Johannesburg. British and German builders supplied these classes of 4-8-2s.

In South Africa, which at one time owned 400 Garratts, the 4-8-2, or Mountain, was by far the most popular type. Two 15AR Class 4-8-2s have their freight train—but not the wind—under control as they blast through Lalisa in 1981.

By the 1930s South Africa was looking to Continental as well as British and American builders to satisfy its demand for modern and more powerful steam locomotives. Chief Mechanical Engineer AG Watson designed and Henschel supplied six 16E Class Pacifics in 1935 (*below*). With a large boiler, poppet-valve cylinders and the largest diameter driving wheels of any narrow gauge locomotive in the world, the 16Es were capable of wheeling expresses along at high speed.

Another Watson design was the 15E Class 4-8-2, which was developed into the 15F, both classes totaling 355. As shown *above*, 15F No 2958, which arrived from North British in 1939, was hard at work with the Ladybrand passenger train in 1983.

Another numerically impressive group of 4-8-2s was the 19 Class, first introduced in 1928. German, Swiss, Czech and British builders supplied 335 of these over a 20-year period. No 2714 (*opposite*) is one of a batch constructed by Borsig on the eve of World War II. Brass and copper embellishments, fitted and paid for by proud crews, characterized many SAR locomotives.

A close cousin of the 19, at least in appearance, was the 24 Class 2-8-4. Supplied by North British for branch line service, the Berkshires remained active through the closing years of steam on South African Railways. In this scene, No 3633 has been paired with 19D No 2719 for working the Maclear-Sterkstroom passenger line.

The most modern steam power in South Africa was the 25 Class 4-8-4. Built by Henschel and North British in 1953-54, these engines had massive boilers, cast steel frames and roller bearings. Two versions were delivered: condensing, for service in the Great Karoo Desert, and non-condensing. One of the former, No 3511 (*opposite*) shows the banjo-shaped extended smokebox, the base of which contains a receiver for cinders.

Because of high maintenance costs, most of the condensing engines were converted to conventional operation. Unfortunate-

ly, once the condensing apparatus had been removed, the tenders were simply cut down to the bare essentials. The result, shown with No 3471 (*opposite, below*) was nicknamed 'bathtub' or 'torpedo.' Final development of the non-condenser was the experimental Red Devil (*below*). The rebuilt 3450, which featured a gas-producer firebox, improved dual exhaust and superheater, and chromium-lined cylinders, was more powerful and efficient than the unmodified engines, but, no matter how economical, steam in South Africa was doomed by dieselization and electrification.

One of the early non-condensing 25s races through Tweespruit, in the Orange Free State, on the kind of rising grade the class could take in stride. No 3419 heads the Bloemfontein-Bethlehem day train.

As in Zimbabwe, many steeply-graded lines in parts of South Africa became Garratt territory. The GF Double Pacifics like No 2378 (*opposite*) were general service engines, their medium-sized wheels and light-axle loading giving them wide flexibility. All units were built in Germany. Beyer Peacock supplied the 50 postwar double Mountain Garratts of class GEA (*opposite, below*). Incredibly, the GEAs, which worked some of the most difficult sections of railroad in the Cape, were hand fired. As such, they were early candidates for withdrawal.

The largest class of Garratts in the world, the GMA/M 40802 + 2-8-4, consisted of 120 engines with cast steel frames and roller bearing axles. They replaced GEAs on the Garden Route, and were themselves made redundant by diesels. The GMA/M survivors, like those from some of the other Garratt classes, were sold to industrial concerns. No 4072 (*this page*) powers a special through Camfer.

As the end of the century draws near, the only future for steam in a country where coal is still a primary resource lies in the coal fields themselves, and even here, diesels are encroaching. Two of Witbank Colliery's 4-8-2s raise the roof as they lift loads upgrade.

ASIA

I ndia is one of the few places left in the world with large concentrations of steam power. Steam construction in the country itself did not cease until 1972, at which time nearly 10,000 locomotives were at work on the broad, meter and narrow gauge lines. True, dieselization, electrification and the retirement of non-standard types has made the steam scene less interesting of late, but the tiny, 2-foot gauge B Class 0-4-0 tanks of the Northeast Frontier Railway's Darjeeling Himalayan line (*right*) are still in use—weather and terrorist attacks permitting.

Also in business, though not with the same exalted status they enjoyed in pre-diesel days, are the magnificent bullet-nosed WP Pacifics (*below*). Built in the United States, Canada, Austria, Poland and India between 1947 and 1967, these 4-6-2s were the Indian Railways' standard postwar passenger and express engines.

One hundred percent steam-operated until recently, the Gwalior system, located just south of Agra, featured outside-frame locomotives of British, Japanese and American origin. Blue-painted NH/4 Class Baldwin 2-8-2 No 756 (*opposite*) is taking coal.

With no indigenous coal resources, neighboring Pakistan chose to dieselize early, relying in the interim on a dwindling fleet of vintage British and wartime Canadian steam power. The classic favorite of British visitors in particular was the graceful inside cylinder SPS Class 4-4-0, which could be found on cross-country locals like the one shown leaving Ajnala in the Punjab. In the late 1980s Pakistan had the world's largest number of active 4-4-0s.

Though hopelessly inefficient, the railways of Indonesia (PJKA) offered a veritable cornucopia of steam right into the 1970s. With a roster of everything from 0-4-0 tanks to 2-8-8-0 Mallets, the island of Java became a mecca for steam fans from all over the globe. In 1981 a wood-burning B52 Class 0-4-0 poses alongside a turn-of-the-century 0-4-2T tram engine at Tegal (*above*).

On Indonesia's Independence Day, a handsome flag-bedecked 4-6-4T (*below*) pauses for liquid refreshment at Tulungagung.

Leaking steam from every joint, a CC50 Class 2-8-8-0 Mallet (*opposite*) has all it can do to lift its own weight up the grade into Cidatar. Blessed (or cursed) with abundant offshore oil deposits, Indonesia chose to buy quantities of diesels, though it is doubtful whether the railways are any less chaotic as a result.

Chanting to the gods in a language only the followers of steam would understand, a 2-8-8-0 Mallet attempts a fair imitation of the volcano looming behind it—which would, in fact, erupt late in 1981, powdering the countryside with fine, white dust.

Negros Island, a paradise for steam worshipers in the Philippines, had ten sugar mills, each with its own colorful narrow gauge antique collection. The Hawaiian-Philippine Company kept its red cabbage-stack 'dragons' in first class condition. Consider 0-6-0 No 4 (*this page*), a Baldwin graduate of 1920.

La Carlota mill preferred lined black for No 102 (*opposite, below*), another Baldwin.

The most decrepit line was the Ma-Ao Central, which had a penchant for running its engines off the tracks. At least yellow Alco Mogul No 5 (*opposite*) was fortunate in being able to cross the river before leaving the rails. Some mill engines burned oil, others *bagasse*, or sugar cane waste, which was packed tightly into bundles and flung into the flames. For anyone craving a taste of short line railroading from 70 years ago and veteran steam power, the 'sugar' roads of Negros Island were sweet indeed.

The Japanese occupation of Taiwan from 1894 to 1945 resulted in a Japanese railroad system, including most of the steam locomotives, until American-built diesels arrived. Both 2-8-0 No DT 613 (*above*) and graceful 4-6-2 No CT 258 (*below*), photographed at Chia-Yi, a junction on the 3-foot, 6-inch gauge west coast main line, were identical to Consolidations and Pacifics on the Japanese National Railways. In fact, when main line steam operations ceased in Japan, fans from that country found the cost of a Tokyo-Taipei air ticket a small price to pay for 2-8-0s, 2-8-2s and 4-6-2s built in the workshops of Hitachi and Mitsubishi.

For something unique, one had to travel to the 2-foot, 6-inch gauge logging line at Ali-Shan. Fifteen tiny, two-truck Shays were allocated here, including No 17 (*opposite*). At least one Shay has been purchased by the Puffing Billy Railway in Australia.

Efficient the Japanese may be, but their high regard for the steam locomotive must have accounted for its survival into the 1970s. Railway enthusiasm is widespread in Japan, just as it is in the industrialized nations of the Western world, and about 500 steam locomotives have been preserved around the country.

In 1973 the islands of Kyushu and Hokkaido were the last bastions of active steam. At Miyazaki C507 Class Pacifics like No 65 (*above*) were holding their own on local passenger trains, while C56 Class Moguls, including No 92 (*below*), which had been brightly polished for hauling the emperor's train, were busy on the branch lines.

In 1971 this D51 Class 2-8-2 with twin headlights (*opposite*) was photographed at Tomakomai Junction, Hokkaido, with a freight from Iwamizawa.

Only one country continued building steam into the 1980s: China. JS Class 2-8-2 No 6015 (*above*), decidedly Soviet in appearance, with ribbed smoke deflectors and partial skyline casing, was one of three newly overhauled locomotives standing in the yard at Changchun, waiting for a shakedown run.

Also with boilers of Soviet design were the RM Class Pacifics of 1957 (*below*). Though being ousted by diesels in other parts of the country, a significant number of RMs were still in use on passenger trains in Northeast China as recently as 1988.

The prize for the most handsome locomotive in China goes to the beautifully proportioned SL, or Victory Class 4-6-2. Fitted with twin headlights and burnished bands around the smokestack, No 664 (*opposite*) departs Bei Shan with a local passenger train. Red wheels and pilots were characteristics of Chinese steam power.

Based on the Soviet Railways' LV Class 2-10-2, the QJ, or Forward Class, was built in large numbers by the Datong locomotive factory until 1988. The QJ was the standard heavy freight engine in China. No 6850 passes Xiao Nan with a freight for Changchun.

AUSTRALIA

The swan song of steam in Australia took place in the early 1970s, during which time a flurry of last runs occurred. Happily, steam never quite died, and the preservation movement is flourishing. Symbolic of steam's longevity is the Victorian Railways' broad gauge R Class 4-6-4 Hudson, built by North British from 1951 (*opposite and below*).

Intended as replacements for older 10-wheelers on express passenger work, the 4-6-4s were soon displaced by diesels. No sooner were the 4-6-4s in service than the first J Class 2-9-0s from Vulcan Foundry in England were being off-loaded. No 515 (*right*) is one of the last steam locomotives in regular service– it endured as a workshop switcher until 1979–and now has found a new role as an excursion engine. In this capacity, it is seen leaving Benalla, heading for Melbourne.

Pride of the standard gauge New South Wales Government Railways was the C38 Class heavy Pacific, built in 1943 by Clyde Engineering in Sydney. When new, the 4-6-2s took over the more important passenger duties from 1925-vintage C36 Class ten-wheelers. A train with which they were associated for many years was the *Newcastle Flyer*, a crack express which was often still steam-powered until 1970. Class leader No 3801 (*opposite*), being serviced at Bathurst, hauled Australia's Bicentennial train in 1988 and starred in an evocative film entitled *A Steam Train Passes*. The partial streamlining applied to the 3801 and four of its classmates was patterned after that of the New Haven Hudsons.

For service around the city, 145 4-6-4 tank locomotives were built by Beyer Peacock and Eveleigh Workshops in Sydney between 1903 and 1917. A number of the C30s, as they were classed, were later converted to 4-6-0 tender locomotives for use on country branch lines, and in that capacity No 3090 (*this page*) is taking an excursion along the Merriwa branch in August 1970.

One of the 4-6-4 tank originals, No 3112 (*opposite, below*) was photographed leading Australia's oldest operating steam locomotive, Z12 Class 4-4-0 No 1210, a veteran of 1878.

Also introduced to replace older steam power, South Australian Railways' broad gauge 620 Class Pacifics, built at the company's own workshops in 1936, were assigned to branch line and suburban passenger services. They were retired in 1969, but two have been spared the torch. No 621 is shown crossing Currency Creek Bridge with an excursion returning from Victor Harbor to Adelaide.

With two water gins and a train of vintage cars returning to Sydney from Melbourne, Nos 1210 and 3112 open up in spectacular fashion at the approach to Bethungra Spiral on the Southern Main Line. In their heyday, the 4-4-0s worked such premier trains as the *Melbourne Express*.

A few last glimpses of Australian steam. Introduced between 1951 and 1958 for express and local passenger work, Queensland Railways' 3-foot, 6-inch gauge BB 18-1/4 4-6-2s were soon relegated by dieselization to less important tasks. Two of the four engines preserved are still in service. No 1072 (*below*) hauls tourist trains on the Lithgow Zig-Zag Railway.

Victorian Railways' K Class 2-8-0, the first of which emerged from Newport Workshops in 1922, were trouble-free maids of all work. One remained on the roster as a shop switcher until 1979. No 153 (*above*) awaits attention at Newport, near Melbourne, prior to working an excursion.

Another member of the class, No 160 (*opposite*), now owned by Castlemaine and Malden Railway, heads an authentic mixed train in October 1988.

The earliest preservation scheme in Australia, the Puffing Billy Railway, deserves special mention. In 1962, enthusiasts reopened a portion of the narrow gauge Gembrook line, east of Melbourne. Since then, tourists from all over the world have flocked to the railway, and trains are packed.

Though the engines built for the line, the Na Class 2-6-2 tanks like No 7A (*above*) predominate, the society also has acquired a Shay from Taiwan and even a Climax (*below*) from the Tyers Valley Tramway, a logging line in southern Victoria. A favored location for photography is Monbulk Creek trestle (*opposite*), being carefully negotiated by Na 8A and Na 7A.

LATIN AMERICA

E ven today, three decades since the Class I railroads of the United States and Canada dispensed with steam power, a few pockets of activity can be found in Latin America. For the most part, railroads south of the Rio Grande relied on American builders, and Mexico even obtained secondhand power from such roads as the Nickel Plate and the Florida East Coast. As late as 1967 4-8-4s built in Schenectady, New York were working from the Valle de Mexico roundhouse near Mexico City, and a handful of the Northerns, plus a few Alco 2-8-0s like No 1150 pictured at El Salto (*right*), have survived.

Still using steam power on a regular basis is the Mexican Pacific of Los Mochis, Sinaloa, where at the height of the sugar harvest in December 1977, No 6, a 1920 Baldwin 2-6-2 once owned by the California Western (*below*), was being fired up alongside No 7, another Prairie from the same builder.

Meanwhile, on the narrow gauge, steam has returned to haul tourist trains. Based at Cuaútla is Baldwin 2-8-0 No 279 (*opposite*), which was slogging upgrade near Cuauhtémoc in August 1987.

Nationalized in 1970, the Guatemalan portion of the International Railways of Central America, owned by the United Fruit Company, inherited most of the modern Krupp, Porter and Baldwin outside-frame Mikados. Though nearly all of the Ferrocarriles de Guatemala steam locomotives have since been retired in favor of diesels, some of the 2-8-2s are kept for emergency use. No 205 shatters the stillness of Escuintla as it shows off for visiting photographers.

For the aficionado of US steam, the cane fields of Cuba had an abundance. At some of the sugar 'centrals' one could even find engines of different gauges working side by side. Such is the case at Central Quentin Banderas (*opposite*), where standard gauge Alco-Cooke 2-6-2 No 1547 rubbed shoulders with No 1230, a Baldwin 2-8-0, built in 1920 and 1919, respectively. In the scene *above*, a Vulcan 2-6-0 of 1917 vintage arrives at Central Abel Santa Maria with freshly cut sugar cane.

The best place to photograph Cuban steam at work was the cane fields themselves. Central Braulio Coroneau's 30-inch gauge Baldwin 2-6-0 No 1338 (*below*) prepares to return to the mill in February 1980.

To find more spectacular, though less frequent, steam activity, one had to travel further south of the Andes. Into the 1980s American-built engines were still earning their keep here. Indeed, a shortage of spares for diesels made the hard-pressed National Railroads of Colombia decide to overhaul Baldwin 2-8-2 No 47 (*opposite*) and others for switching duties.

Other Baldwins were to be seen gainfully employed in Ecuador and Peru. Guayaquil & Quito Railway 2-8-0 No 53 (*above*), built as recently as 1953, is taking water at Sibambe before climbing the Devil's Nose switchbacks, and Ferrocarril Huancayo-Huancavelica 2-6-0 No 103 (*below*) is providing hot water for the villagers at Telleria.

Perhaps the most impressive Baldwins in all of South America were the Bolivian National Railways' 2-10-2s. The mighty Santa Fes were hauling freight on the Uyuni-Atocha-Villazon section as late as December 1976. This picture, showing No 705 on the Altiplano near Huari, was taken by asking the crew to provide smoke, walking a mile up the track, running alongside the engine as it passed and jumping aboard before it picked up speed.

The broad gauge system in Southern Chile offered coal-burning steam power from a diversity of manufacturers–American, British, European, Japanese and Chilean. This ten-wheeler (*above*), shuffling away from Valdivia after a rain shower, came from Scotland in 1908. Mikado No 750 (*opposite*), erupting out of a Temuco yard on a freight to Osorno, was built by Alco in 1925. Mitsubishi supplied 4-8-2 No 354 (*below*) in 1952. Substituting for a failed diesel, the hefty mountain type is leaving Cajon with the daily northbound, all-stations local. Parts of these 4-8-2s were interchangeable with those of earlier Baldwin engines in the same series.

Argentina, with its multiplicity of gauges (five) and an incredible assortment of steam locomotives from all over the world, was a 'must' for any South American steam odyssey. British-built standard gauge 4-6-0 No 234 (*opposite*) of the FC General Urquiza was in charge of a short local passenger train at Goya in 1975.

Meter gauge FC General Belgrano 2-6-2 No 4606 (*below*), built in Switzerland, was switching at Santa Fe a year later.

The FC General Roca had two gauges: 5-foot, 6-inch on the Pampa and 75 cm in the less hospitable wilds of Patagonia. The *Old Patagonian Express* is the unofficial name given by author Paul Theroux to this train, otherwise known as the daily Esquel branch mixed. Baldwin No 20 and Henschel No 130, both Mikados, are striding across the high desert with the northbound train (*above*), which in 1976 featured a diner serving steak and wine.

Even today Paraguay's standard gauge Presidente Antonio Lopez Railway maintains a fleet of wood-burning engines. The poor condition of the track is the reason why diesels have so far failed to make any inroads. Instead, Paraguay has resorted to obtaining redundant steam engines from Argentina in order to operate any semblance of service. One of the first locomotives built for the line, a 2-6-0 No 60 built in 1910, stops at Coronel Bogado with the southbound International train, conveying a through coach for Bueños Aires.

Although the Federal Railways of Brazil (RFFSA) had been extensively dieselized and electrified by the mid-1970s, enough steam power remains to make a visit there worthwhile. The Durango of Brazil is São João del Rey, where the 2-foot, 6-inch gauge railroad has become an operating museum, featuring elderly outside-frame Baldwin 4-4-0s, 2-8-0s and 4-6-0s. Polished and decorated Consolidation No 55 (*opposite*) dates from 1892.

Among the industrial railroads relying on steam were the Portland Cement Company, which owned a 60 cm gauge line near São Paulo. No 7 (*above*), a Porter 2-6-2 built in 1945, is bringing a load of stone into the yard at Cajamar.

Brazil's sugar *usinas* also provided a wealth of interesting engines, some of which previously saw service on the main lines. Wood-burning meter gauge 2-8-0 No 5 (*below*), a diamond-stack Baldwin built in 1894, is shoving loads of sugar cane into the Usina Barcelos near Campos.

NORTH AMERICA

In decline elsewhere, steam in North America, as in Britain, has enjoyed a renaissance. Though confined to excursions, museums and tourist lines, steam locomotives are attracting a new generation of admirers who never knew steam in regular service.

Fortunately, one of the major transcontinental railroads, the Union Pacific, is represented by a sizable selection of steam locomotives, both large and small. A number of 0-6-0 switchers were saved, among which was No 4466 (*right*), the last of its class to lug and shove cars around the yard in Cheyenne, Wyoming.

Built for long distance fast freight and passenger traffic, FEF3 Class 4-8-4 No 8444 (*below*) is probably the world's most famous excursion engine. In fact, the four-digit Northern has spent nearly three decades hauling fan trips. Doubleheading with Challenger 4-6-6-4 No 3985 over Southern Pacific tracks through Donner Pass, California, the big 4-8-4 is seen heading home following a visit to the Sacramento Rail Fair in 1981.

A closer look at the massive, employee-restored articulated (*opposite*), shown turning on the wye at Laramie, Wyoming, illustrates well Union Pacific's slogan 'We can handle it.'

Like their 4-8-4 stablemates, the Challengers were equally at home on freight or passenger work. With a comparatively light-weight excursion of 10 cars, the 3985 sails effortlessly up Sherman Hill, bound for Cheyenne.

Deservedly the most famous of all tourist railroads in the United States, the Strasburg, located in the heart of Pennsylvania Dutch country, boasts a fine selection of steam power, from a former Canadian National 0-6-0 (*below*), to a sturdy 2-10-0 (*opposite, below*). Originally the star of a small steam fleet belonging to the Great Western Railway, a sugar beet hauler in Loveland, Colorado, the Decapod is a regular performer on the Strasburg's Fridays-only mixed train. The main attraction at Strasburg, however, has been the occasional doubleheading of two locomotives from the Pennsylvania Railroad Museum collection. Teaming up for the first time in October 1983, E7s 4-4-2 No 7002 and D6sb 4-4-0 No 1223 (*opposite*) put on an impressive display of smoke and steam as they storm away from Carpenters, Pennsylvania.

Though the railroad itself has become part of the giant Burlington Northern System, the Northern Pacific lives on, thanks to its preserved steam locomotives. Two Northern Pacific engines, which operate from time to time, are shown here. The L9 0-6-0s were the most numerous yard goats on the roster. No 1070 (*above and opposite*), delivered by Alco in 1907, now works for the Lake Whatcom Railway in Washington State. From the same builder in the same year came this S10 Class ten-wheeler (*below*). Intended for the South Manchurian Railway, the 328 and its classmates were ideally suited for branch line, mixed and freight service because of their small (57-inch diameter) driving wheels. This engine is owned by the Minnesota Transportation Museum.

The Norfolk & Western believed that its locomotives should burn what they hauled—coal—which explains why the N&W kept building steam power long after other railroads had embraced newer technology. Sophisticated and efficient, the railroad's big three—J Class 4-8-4, A Class 2-6-6-4 and Y6b Class 2-8-8-2—held the diesels at bay until 1959. The last A articulated, No 1218 (opposite) towers above the photographer at Columbus, Ohio, after arriving with a freight from Portsmouth.

The streamlined J, No 611 (right), speeds through Falwell, Virginia with one of its first revenue runs following restoration in 1982.

These superpower machines were built at the N&W's own locomotive factory in Roanoke and restored for excursion duties in the 1980s. Side by side (below), both engines take possession of the double-track main through Christiansburg, Virginia. Parallel running was the highlight of the 1987 NRHS Convention.

As late as 1967, it was possible to see narrow gauge Baldwin 2-8-2s powering freights through the Rockies; indeed, these became the last regular steam operations on a major United States railroad. Fortunately, enough remains of the Rio Grande's once-extensive 3-foot gauge system in Colorado and New Mexico to give one an appreciation of the glory that used to be.

Its immaculate condition belying its age, 107-year-old 2-8-0 No 346 is fired up a few times each year at the Colorado Railroad Museum in Golden, Colorado *(above)*. A youngster by comparison is outside-frame K28 Class 2-8-2 No 473 of 1923 vintage *(below)*.

Fitted with a snowplow, the Mikado works the scenic Silverton branch from Durango. Recreating a scene from the not-so-distant past, a larger 2-8-2 of class K36 *(opposite)* pauses at the Cresco water tank with a special photographer's freight bound for Cumbres Pass.

On the climb from Chama to the 10,015 foot summit of Cumbres Pass, doubleheading and/or pushing was the rule. Lengthy trains often had the helper cut in halfway, because the weight of two engines together was too much for the Lobato trestle. Here, twin 2-8-2s blacken an otherwise clear sky above Chama. As late as 1967 it was possible to see tandem 2-8-2s powering freights. Indeed, these became the last regular steam-powered operations on a major US railroad.

Canada was a last stronghold of steam in North America, and when the Canadian National and Canadian Pacific dieselized in 1961, a number of locomotives that would otherwise have met the torch found new homes in the United States. At one stage there were more ex-Canadian National and Canadian Pacific engines at work below the Canadian border than in the dominion itself.

Wearing the number plate of its former owner, as well as its new number, 0-18 a Class 0-6-0 No 7470 (*opposite*) eases out of the roundhouse at North Conway, New Hampshire.

A glimpse of G-3h Pacific No 2317 (*left*) was enough to bring tears to the eyes of any CPR fan. Newly restored in 1978 and freshly painted in the CPR's traditional passenger livery of maroon, gold and gunmetal gray, the 4-6-2 is part of the late Nelson Blount's Steamtown Vermont collection.

The Canadian Pacific Railroad owned a total of 498 4-6-2s. Considered dual service engines, they were used all over the system, on both passenger and freight trains. The last one (*below*) was also the last engine built by the CPR's own Angus Shops. In November 1985 the G5 traveled from its home at the Museum of Science and Technology in Ottawa to Western Canada, where it hauled a 'Last Spike' commemorative train from Revelstoke to Craigellachie, British Columbia, marking the 100th anniversary of the completion of the transcontinental main line.

Alas, historically accurate restoration cannot be used to describe the other locomotives operating on the main lines of the Canadian West. Among the engines to suffer the excesses of commercialism is former CPR H-1 e 4-6-4 *Royal Hudson* No 2860, which now sports a collection of plates and plaques that mar its handsome appearance. Classmate No 2850 hauled the Royal Train across Canada in 1939, and royal permission was given to name this and the other engines in the series *Royal Hudsons*. Accordingly, these partially streamlined 4-6-4s were fitted with embossed crowns. Despite the accumulation of metal bric-a-brac added during, and following, restoration in 1974, the 2860 manages to retain an air of dignity as it marches through Shannon, British Columbia.

In the United States, the South accounted for both a revival of main line steam and some of the last short line steam operations in the country. Typical of rural steam railroading in Dixie was the Mississippian Railway, which owned two Ex-Frisco 2-8-0s. One of them, No 77 (*below*), is shown rolling along a grass-covered right-of-way near Smithville, Mississippi.

A little more elegant, perhaps, is the ex-Savannah & Atlanta 4-6-2 No 750 (*opposite, below*), which helped usher in a new steam era on the all-diesel Southern Railway. Seen at Emory Gap, Tennessee with an Autumn Foliage Special from Chattanooga to Crossville, the trim Pacific requires the assistance of two FP7 diesels to maintain the schedule of its heavy train.

Another 4-6-2 to return to the high iron is No 152 (*opposite*), the Louisville & Nashville's sole surviving steam locomotive. Owned by the Kentucky Railroad Museum, this lanky Pacific also has a diesel in attendance for the grades, such as this one near Ford, Kentucky.

At one time, the steam fleet of the mighty Southern Pacific was the most varied anywhere. From home-built 0-6-0s to sleek, stream-styled 4-8-4s and massive, cab-forward 4-8-8-2s, the Southern Pacific was a locomotive historian's delight. Fortunately, around 40 Southern Pacific engines escaped destruction, and a few are kept in working order. S10 Class 0-6-0 No 1269 (*above*), now owned by the Pacific Locomotive Association, spent many years as a switcher at Oakland, California.

M6 Class 2-6-0 (*below*), typical of Southern Pacific branch line and way freight power, was based at Sacramento, California.

The glamour award, however, goes to GS4 4-8-4 No 4449 (*opposite*). Built by Lima in 1941 to haul the Southern Pacific's *Daylight* streamliner between San Francisco and Los Angeles, the Northern was selected for the American Freedom Train Bicentennial tour of 1975-76. The superpower 4-8-4 is shown blasting toward the summit of Rice Hill, on Southern Pacific's Siskiyou line.

If any one engine can be credited with bringing the Age of Steam to life in the South once again, it is this Mikado: the legendary 4501. Originally intended for hauling freight, the 2-8-2 was painted in Southern Railway's passenger paint scheme of green and gold and used on system-wide excursions beginning in 1966. The wooden trestle across Lake Ponchartrain, Louisiana is the setting for this portrait of steam in the South.

Years ago, the forests of the Pacific Northwest echoed to the sound of steam whistles. Most of the locomotives and the logging railroads that operated them have long since disappeared, but the whistles still linger. Crossing the Nisqually River Bridge near Elbe, Washington, ex-Port of Grays Harbor No 5, a conventional Porter 2-8-2 built in 1924 stirs memories of a bygone era with a train of empty log cars.

180

With such a scarcity of steam on the principal railroads of the West, it is not surprising that interest has turned to short line engines, quite a number of which have been restored to operating condition. McCloud River Railroad's Alco 2-6-2 No 25 (*below*), custom-built to haul logs and lumber products, forms the centerpiece of this timeless scene: railroading as it used to be.

In the San Francisco Bay Area, a group of enthusiasts called the Pacific Locomotive Association has assembled a fine collection of engines from various California short lines. No 12 (*opposite*), built in 1903 for the Sierra Railroad, is one of the oldest operating Shays in existence. No 4 is a 1924 Baldwin 2-6-6-2T, which was used by the Clover Valley Lumber Company.

A favorite among rail fans has always been the Sierra itself. Two of the line's stalwarts (*opposite, below*), Rogers 4-6-0 No 3, built in 1891, and Baldwin 2-8-0 No 28, built in 1922, doublehead up Montezuma Hill with a train of Harriman cars bound for Jamestown, California.

Undoubtedly the most versatile of all freight engines was the 2-8-2, or Mikado type. A grand total of 10,000 were built for lines in the United States. The 2-8-2, with its small diameter driving wheels and large firebox, could be used on freight drags or for heavy switching. Nickel Plate Mike No 587, one of the 1266 USRA light 2-8-2s built from 1918 on, survived until the very end of steam. Fitted with a tender from a scrapped Berkshire, the 587 is shown pulling away from Camden, Indiana, with a train made up primarily of ex-Santa Fe and Burlington stainless steel cars.

Beginning in 1925 Lima Locomotive Works of Lima, Ohio became synonymous with superpower steam when an experimental 'extended Mikado,' with a larger firebox and a four-wheeled, booster-fitted trailing truck, entered service with the Boston & Albany Railroad. This 2-8-4, or Berkshire type, revolutionized railroading by combining power and speed in one locomotive. From 1925 until 1948 an array of superpower engines emerged from the Lima factory: 2-10-4s, like Texas & Pacific's No 610 (*above*); 2-8-4s, including Nickel Plate 765 (*opposite*); 2-8-8-8-4s for the Southern Pacific; 2-6-6-6s for the Chesapeake & Ohio; and 4-8-4s, culminating in the C&O J3 Greenbrier, exemplified by No 614 (*below*), the last steam locomotive to be commercially built in the United States. To see and hear a Lima product thundering upgrade was an unforgettable experience.

Superpower in action. Leaving behind the remnants of a February storm, Lima 4-8-4 No 614 of the C&O, its pilot encrusted with snow, blasts through Scott Depot, West Virginia, with coal empties bound for Huntington.

One of the most remarkable operating museums anywhere in North America is the Mid-Continent Museum at North Freedom, Wisconsin. A pleasing blend of authentic restoration and the atmosphere of a 1920s era branch line enables visitors to travel back to a time when steam ruled the rails of North America, and the rest of the world as well. Chicago & Northwestern ten-wheeler No 1385, built in 1907 (*below*), is ready to depart for Quartzite Lake with the kind of train for which it was designed.

Even more becoming is Dardanelle & Russelville 2-6-0 No 9 (*left*), a Baldwin built in 1884, laying down the smoke at La Rue.

The museum's annual doubleheaded snow train gives steam a chance to be truly spectacular. In the scene *opposite*, ex-Western Coal & Coke No 1, a Montreal-built ten-wheeler, sends up geysers of steam into the frosty air, stealing the show from its teammate, ex-Saginaw Timber No 2, a 1912 Baldwin 2-8-2.

Remember when railroading used to be like this?

INDEX

Allegheny (2-6-6-6) 187
American (4-4-0) 15, 111, 129, 133, 155, 161
Atlantic (4-4-2) 45, 161
Austrian State Railways (OBB) 57
Barton Wright (0-6-0) 9
Belgian State Railways (SNCB) 45
Belpaire Boiler 12
Berkshire (2-8-4) 72, 76, 98, 187
Beyer Peacock 87, 91, 104, 129
Bluebell Railway 15
Bolivian National Railway 147
Borsig 96
Boston & Albany Railroad 187
British Railways 9, 15, 16, 18, 22, 24, 30, 34, 38, 42
Bulgarian State Railways (BDZ) 72
Bulleid, OV 40
Burlington Northern Railroad 162
Canadian National 170
Canadian Pacific 170
Castlemaine & Malden Railway 135
Challenger (4-6-6-4) 6, 158-159
Chapelon, André 45, 71
Chesapeake (2-8-8-2) 165
Chesapeake & Ohio Railroad 187-188
Chicago & Northwestern Railroad 190
Chruchward, GJ 20
Climax 136
Clover Valley Lumber Company 183
Collett, Charles 20
Consolidation (2-8-0) 30, 47, 58, 70, 81, 82, 135, 139, 143, 145, 155, 166, 175, 183, 190
Czechoslovakian State Railways (ČSD) 71
Dardenelle & Russelville Railroad 190
Dean Goods (0-6-0) 10
Decapod (2-10-0) 45, 65, 76, 81, 82, 83, 161
Denmark State Railways (DSB) 58
East German Railways (DR) 62, 65-66
E Class 0-10-0 76
Eveleigh Workshops 129

Federal Railways of Brazil (RFFSA) 155
Finnish State Railways (VR) 60
4-8-8-4 176
Franco-Crosti boiler 47
French National Railroads (SNCF) 45
Garratt 87, 88, 91, 92, 95, 104
German Federal Railways (DB) 62, 65, 66, 72
Giesl ejector 57
Golsdorf, Karl 57
Grange 20
Great Eastern Railway 52
Great Southern & Western Railway 9
Great Western Railway (Colorado) 161
Greenbrier (4-8-4) 187-188
Gresley, Sir Nigel 16, 33
Guayaqil & Quito Railway 145
Hall 20
Halsingbörg-Hasselehölm Railway 58
Hedjaz Railway 87
Hellenic State Railways 81
Hendrie, DA 92
Hudson (4-6-4) 88, 91, 127, 129, 172
Hungary State Railways (MAV) 75
Indian Railway 109
Indonesian Railways (PJKA) 112
International Railways 140
Italian State Railways (FS) 47
Ivatt, BJ 18
J Class 2-9-0 127
Keighley & Worth Valley Railway 12, 29
Kent & East Sussex Railway 12
King 20, 21
King Arthur 4-6-0 15, 24, 26
Kriegslok 2-1-0 57
Lancashire & Yorkshire Railway (L&Y) 9
Lake Whatcom Railway 162
Lima Locomotove Works 187
London & North Eastern Railway 16
London & Southwestern Railway 24
London Midland & Scottish Railway (LMS) 9, 16, 29, 36, 42

Louisville & Nashville Railroad 174
Ma-Ao Central Railroad 117
McCloud River Railroad 183
Manor 20
Mid-Hants Railway 15, 24
Midland Railway (MR) 9, 12, 30
Mikado (2-8-2) 30, 45, 49, 75, 82, 89, 91, 109, 118, 121, 122, 140, 145, 148, 151, 166, 169, 178, 180, 184
Mississippian Railway 174
Modified Hall 20
Mogul (2-6-0) 16, 18, 20, 58, 117, 121, 143, 145, 153, 176
Mountain (4-8-2) 45, 71, 72, 91, 92, 95, 96, 104, 107, 149
National Railway of Zimbabwe (NRZ) 91
New South Wales Government Railways 129
Newport Workshops 135
Northeast Frontier Railway 109
Norfolk & Western Railroad 165
Northern (4-8-4) 6, 78, 101, 139, 157, 165, 176
North Yorkshire Moors Railway 16
North British 98, 101, 127
Northern Pacific Railroad 162
Norwegian State Railways (NSB) 58
0-4-4-0 52
0-4-0 109, 112
0-6-0 12, 30, 117, 157, 161-162, 170, 176
Pacific (4-6-2) 6, 33, 36, 40, 45, 62, 66, 75, 87-88, 92, 96, 104, 109, 118, 121, 122, 129, 130, 135, 170, 174
Pacific Locomotive Association 176, 183
P8 4-6-0 68, 72
Peppercorn, AH 16
Polish State Railways (PKP) 68, 71
Portuguese Railway Company (CP) 52
Prairie (2-6-2) 62, 75-76, 91, 136, 139, 143, 151, 155, 183
Presidente Carlos Antonio Lopez Railway 153
Prussian Railways (KPEV) 62, 65, 72

P36 4-8-4 78
Puffing Billy Railway 136
Queensland Railway 135
Rio Grande Railroad 166
Romanian State Railways (CFR) 72
Saint 20
Santa Fe (2-10-2) 75-76, 81, 124, 147
Saxon-Meyer (0-4-4-0T) 65
Saxon State Railways 65
Severn Valley Railway 10, 18, 20, 42
Shay 118, 136, 183
Sierra Railroad 183
South African Railways (SAR) 92, 96, 98
South Australian Railway 130
Southern Pacific Railroad 156, 176, 187
Southern Railways (Great Britain) 15, 24, 40
Southern Railways (United States) 174, 178
South Manchurian Railway 162
Soviet Railways (SZD) 76, 124
Spanish State Railways (RENFE) 49
SPS Class 4-4-0 110
Stanier, Sir William 29, 30, 36
Swedish State Railways (SJ) 58
Swiss Federal Railway (SBB) 57
Ten-wheeler (4-6-0) 20, 24, 29, 33, 42, 53, 58, 62, 129, 148, 151, 155, 162, 183, 190
Texas & Pacific Railroad 187
Triplex (2-8-8-8-4) 187
Turkish State Railways (TCUD) 81, 82
2-8-8-0 112, 115
2-6-6-4 165
2-6-6-2T 183
2-6-2T 16
2-10-4 187
Tyers Valley Tramway 136
Union Pacific Railroad 157
Victorian Railways 127, 135
VR3 60
Vulcan Foundry 127
Watson, AG 96
Yugoslavian Railways (JĎZ) 75

BIBLIOGRAPHY

Berkman, Pamela *The History of the Atchison, Topeka & Santa Fe*
Cahill, Marie and Lynne Piade, eds *The History of the Union Pacific: America's Great Transcontinental Railroad*
Casserley, HC *The Observer's Book of British Steam Locomotives*
Christian, Roy and Ken Mills *World of South American Steam*
Clark, Peter *Locomotives in China*
Collins, Joe G *The Search for Steam*
Cook, Richard J *Super Power Steam Locomotives*
Durrant, AE *The Steam Locomotives of Eastern Europe*
Durrant, AE, with CP Lewis and AA Jorgensen *Steam in Africa*
Durrant, AE, with CP Lewis and AA Jorgensen *Steam on the Veld*
Eliot, Jane *The History of Western Railroads*
Gammell, CJ *Relics of the Raj*
Jacobs, Timothy, ed *The History of the Baltimore & Ohio: America's First Railroad*
Jacobs, Timothy *The History of the Pennsylvania Railroad*
Kalla-Bishop, PM *Italian State Railways Steam Locomotives*
Klein, Aaron *The Encyclopedia of North American Railroads*
Le Fleming, HM and JH Price *Russian Steam Locomotives*

Lotz, Jim *The History of the Canadian Pacific*
Lotz, Jim and Keith MacKenzie *Railways of Canada*
McDonnell, Greg *The History of Canadian Railroads*
Oberg, Leon *Locomotives of Australia*
Ransome-Wallis, P *The Last Steam Locomotives of British Railways*
Ransome-Wallis, P *The Last Steam Locomotives of Eastern Europe*
Ransome-Wallis, P *The Last Steam Locomotives of Western Europe*
Smith, AW and DE Bourne *Spirit of Steam*
Talbot, E *Steam from Kenya to the Cape*
Talbot, E *Steam in Turkey*
Wood, Charles R *The Northern Pacific—Main Street of the Northwest*
Yenne, Bill, ed *The History of North American Railroads*
Yenne, Bill *The History of the Southern Pacific*
York, Thomas *America's Great Railroads*
Ziel, Ron and George Foster *Steam in the Sixties*
Ziel, Ron and Mike Eagleson *The Twilight of World Steam*